Life Lessons
from THE INSPIRED WORD of GOD

BOOK of HEBREWS

MAX LUCADO
General Editor

LIFE LESSONS FROM THE INSPIRED WORD OF GOD—BOOK OF HEBREWS

Scripture passages taken from:

The Holy Bible, *New Century Version*

The Holy Bible, *New King James Version*

All excerpts used by permission.

Design and cover art—by Koechel Peterson and Associates, Inc., Minneapolis, Minnesota.

Produced with the assistance of the Livingstone Corporation.

ISBN: 08499-5301-4
Published by W Publishing Group

TABLE OF CONTENTS

HOW TO STUDY THE BIBLE

BY MAX LUCADO

This is a peculiar book you are holding. Words crafted in another language. Deeds done in a distant era. Events recorded in a far-off land. Counsel offered to a foreign people. This is a peculiar book.

It's surprising that anyone reads it. It's too old. Some of its writings date back five thousand years. It's too bizarre. The book speaks of incredible floods, fires, earthquakes, and people with supernatural abilities. It's too radical. The Bible calls for undying devotion to a carpenter who called himself God's Son.

Logic says this book shouldn't survive. Too old, too bizarre, too radical.

The Bible has been banned, burned, scoffed, and ridiculed. Scholars have mocked it as foolish. Kings have branded it as illegal. A thousand times over it the grave has been dug and the dirge has begun, but somehow the Bible never stays in the grave. Not only has it survived, it has thrived. It is the single most popular book in all of history. It has been the best-selling book in the world for years!

There is no way on earth to explain it. Which perhaps is the only explanation. The answer? The Bible's durability is not found on earth; it is found in heaven. For the millions who have tested its claims and claimed its promises, there is but one answer—the Bible is God's book and God's voice.

As you read it, you would be wise to give some thought to two questions. What is the purpose of the Bible? and How do I study the Bible? Time spent reflecting on these two issues will greatly enhance your Bible study.

What is the purpose of the Bible?

Let the Bible itself answer that question.

Since you were a child you have known the Holy Scriptures which are able to make you wise. And that wisdom leads to salvation through faith in Christ Jesus.

(2 Tim. 3:15)

The purpose of the Bible? Salvation. God's highest passion is to get his children home. His book, the Bible, describes his plan of salvation. The purpose of the Bible is to proclaim God's plan and passion to save his children.

That is the reason this book has endured through the centuries. It dares to tackle the toughest questions about life: Where do I go after I die? Is there a God? What do I do with my fears? The Bible offers answers to these crucial questions. It is the treasure map that leads us to God's highest treasure, eternal life.

But how do we use the Bible? Countless copies of Scripture sit unread on bookshelves and nightstands simply because people don't know how to read it. What can we do to make the Bible real in our lives?

The clearest answer is found in the words of Jesus.

"Ask," he promised, *"and God will give it to you. Search and you will find. Knock, and the door will open for you."*

(Matt. 7:7)

The first step in understanding the Bible is asking God to help us. We should read prayerfully. If anyone understands God's Word, it is because of God and not the reader.

But the Helper will teach you everything and will cause you to remember all that I told you. The Helper is the Holy Spirit whom the Father will send in my name.

(John 14:24)

Before reading the Bible, pray. Invite God to speak to you. Don't go to Scripture looking for your idea, go searching for his.

Not only should we read the Bible prayerfully, we should read it carefully. *Search and you will find* is the pledge. The Bible is not a newspaper to be skimmed but rather a mine to be quarried. *Search for it like silver, and hunt for it like hidden treasure. Then you will understand respect for the* Lord, *and you will find that you know God* (Prov. 2:4).

Any worthy find requires effort. The Bible is no exception. To understand the Bible you don't have to be brilliant, but you must be willing to roll up your sleeves and search.

Be a worker who is not ashamed and who uses the true teaching in the right way.

(2 Tim. 2:15)

Here's a practical point. Study the Bible a bit at a time. Hunger is not satisfied by eating twenty-one meals in one sitting once a week. The body needs a steady diet to remain strong. So does the soul. When God sent food to his people in the wilderness, he didn't provide loaves already made. Instead, he sent them manna in the shape of *thin flakes, like frost . . . on the desert ground* (Exod. 16:14).

God gave manna in limited portions.

God sends spiritual food the same way. He opens the heavens with just enough nutrients for today's hunger. He provides, *a command here, a command there. A rule here, a rule there. A little lesson here, a little lesson there* (Isa. 28:10).

Don't be discouraged if your reading reaps a small harvest. Some days a lesser portion is all that is needed. What is important is to search every day for that day's message. A steady diet of God's Word over a lifetime builds a healthy soul and mind.

A little girl returned from her first day at school. Her mom asked, "Did you learn anything?" "Apparently not enough," the girl responded, "I have to go back tomorrow and the next day and the next. . . ."

Such is the case with learning. And such is the case with Bible study. Understanding comes little by little over a lifetime.

There is a third step in understanding the Bible. After the asking and seeking comes the knocking. After you ask and search, then knock.

Knock, and the door will open for you.
(Matt. 7:7)

To knock is to stand at God's door. To make yourself available. To climb the steps, cross the porch, stand at the doorway, and volunteer. Knocking goes beyond the realm of thinking and into the realm of acting.

To knock is to ask, What can I do? How can I obey? Where can I go?

It's one thing to know what to do. It's another to do it. But for those who do it, those who choose to obey, a special reward awaits them.

The truly happy are those who carefully study God's perfect law that makes people free, and they continue to study it. They do not forget what they heard, but they obey what God's teaching says. Those who do this will be made happy.

(James 1:25)

What a promise. Happiness comes to those who do what they read! It's the same with medicine. If you only read the label but ignore the pills, it won't help. It's the same with food. If you only read the recipe but never cook, you won't be fed. And it's the same with the Bible. If you only read the words but never obey, you'll never know the joy God has promised.

Ask. Search. Knock. Simple, isn't it? Why don't you give it a try? If you do, you'll see why you are holding the most remarkable book in history.

HEBREWS

INTRODUCTION

The best just got better—it's a favorite slogan with advertisers.

It's not that our previous product was poor. It's just that the current one is superior.

The Book of Hebrews might well use the same slogan. The best just got better.

There was nothing inferior about the Jewish religion. It was given by God and designed by God. Every principle, rule, and ritual had a wealth of meaning. The Old Testament served as a faithful guide for thousands of people over thousands of years. It was the best offered to man.

But when Christ came, the best got better.

Hebrews was written for Jewish believers who were torn between their new faith and their old ways. The temptation was to slip back into familiar routines and rituals, settling for second best.

The author skillfully makes a case against such a digression. He argues that Jesus is better than every form of the old faith—better than the angels (1:1–2:18), better than their leaders (3:1–4:13), and better than their priests (4:14–7:28). When it comes to comparing the two there is simply no comparison. Christianity has a better covenant (8:1–13), a better sanctuary, (9:1–10), and a better sacrifice for sins (9:11–10:18).

It's not that the old law was bad, it's just that the new law—salvation by faith in Christ—is better. Once you've known the best, why settle for second rate?

It's doubtful that you will ever be tempted to exchange your faith for an ancient system of priests and sacrifices. But you will be tempted to exchange it for something inferior.

If you are reading Hebrews, be reminded: Once you've known the best, why settle for anything less? (Hmmm, there's another catchy slogan.)

LESSON ONE

JESUS UNDERSTANDS US

REFLECTION

Begin your study by sharing thoughts on this question.

1. Where do you usually turn for comfort when you are hurting?

_____

_____

_____

BIBLE READING

Read Hebrews 2:10–18 from the NCV or the NKJV.

NCV

[10]God is the One who made all things, and all things are for his glory. He wanted to have many children share his glory, so he made the One who leads people to salvation perfect through suffering.

[11]Jesus, who makes people holy, and those who are made holy are from the same family.

NKJV

[10]For it was fitting for Him, for whom are all things and by whom are all things, in bringing many sons to glory, to make the captain of their salvation perfect through sufferings. [11]For both He who sanctifies and those who are being sanctified are all of one, for which reason He is not ashamed to call them brethren, [12]saying:

NCV

So he is not ashamed to call them his brothers and sisters. [12]He says,

"Then, I will tell my fellow Israelites about you;

I will praise you in the public meeting."

[13]He also says,

"I will trust in God."

And he also says,

"I am here, and with me are the children God has given me."

[14]Since these children are people with physical bodies, Jesus himself became like them. He did this so that, by dying, he could destroy the one who has the power of death—the devil—[15]and free those who were like slaves all their lives because of their fear of death. [16]Clearly, it is not angels that Jesus helps, but the people who are from Abraham. [17]For this reason Jesus had to be made like his brothers in every way so he could be their merciful and faithful high priest in service to God. Then Jesus could bring forgiveness for their sins. [18]And now he can help those who are tempted, because he himself suffered and was tempted.

NKJV

"I will declare Your name to My brethren;

In the midst of the assembly I will sing praise to You."

[13]And again:

"I will put My trust in Him."

And again:

"Here am I and the children whom God has given Me."

[14]Inasmuch then as the children have partaken of flesh and blood, He Himself likewise shared in the same, that through death He might destroy him who had the power of death, that is, the devil, [15]and release those who through fear of death were all their lifetime subject to bondage. [16]For indeed He does not give aid to angels, but He does give aid to the seed of Abraham. [17]Therefore, in all things He had to be made like His brethren, that He might be a merciful and faithful High Priest in things pertaining to God, to make propitiation for the sins of the people. [18]For in that He Himself has suffered, being tempted, He is able to aid those who are tempted.

DISCOVERY

Explore the Bible reading by discussing these questions.

2. Why did God allow his Son to suffer?

_____

_____

_____

3. What effect did Jesus' victory over death have on Satan?

_____

_____

_____

4. What can free people from their fear of death?

_____

_____

_____

5. Why is Jesus the perfect high priest for us?

_____

_____

_____

6. In what ways is Jesus able to help us?

_____

_____

_____   _____

INSPIRATION

Here is an uplifting thought from the *Inspirational Study Bible.*

It is an undeniable fact that usually it is those who have suffered most who are best able to comfort others who are passing through suffering. I know of pastors whose ministries have been enriched by suffering. Through their trials they have learned to "live through" the difficulties of the people in their parish. They are able to empathize as well as sympathize with the afflictions of others because of what they have experienced in their own lives.

Our sufferings may be rough and hard to bear, but they teach us lessons which in turn equip and enable us to help others. Our attitude toward suffering should not be, "Grit your teeth and bear it," hoping it will pass as quickly as possible. Rather, our goal should be to learn all we can from what we are called upon to endure, so that we can fulfill a ministry of comfort—as Jesus did. "Because he himself suffered when he was tempted, he is able to help those who are being tempted" (Hebrews 2:18, NIV). The sufferer becomes the comforter or helper in the service of the Lord.

By the way, by "enduring" suffering, God led me to my wonderful wife, Ruth, who was His intended one for me.

(from *Unto the Hills*
by Billy Graham)

RESPONSE

Use these questions to share more deeply with each other.

7. How is Jesus' pain and temptation relevant to us?

_____

_____

_____

8. In times of trouble, why do we turn to other people rather than to Jesus?

_____

_____

_____

9. In what way does God equip us to reach out to others with compassion?

_____

_____

_____

PRAYER

Lord, we stand in awe of you for what you have done—you left your throne to live among us, you faced temptation, ridicule, and shame so that you could understand us, and then you died on a cross to save us from our sins. You gave up everything so that we could spend eternity with you. Help us to grasp the depth of your love. And as we experience your great love for us, help us to share it with others.

JOURNALING

Take a few moments to record your personal insights from this lesson.

How has Jesus shown his love for me? How can I thank him?

ADDITIONAL QUESTIONS

10. How should Christians respond to the pain that comes their way?

_____

_____

_____

11. How has knowing God increased your sensitivity and compassion for others?

_____

_____

_____

12. What can you do to show God's love to someone who is hurting?

_____

_____

_____

For more Bible passages about Jesus' ability to help hurting people, see Job 36:15; Psalm 46:1; 121:1, 2; 147:1–5; Isaiah 41:10; 53:3–5; Romans 8:26, 27.

To complete the book of Hebrews during this twelve-part study, read Hebrews 1:1–2:18.

ADDITIONAL THOUGHTS

LESSON TWO

KEEP THE FAITH

REFLECTION

Begin your study by sharing thoughts on this question.

1. Think of a time when a Christian friend encouraged your faith. What did this person do to help you?

_____

_____

_____

BIBLE READING

Read Hebrews 3:1–14 from the NCV or the NKJV.

NCV

¹So all of you holy brothers and sisters, who were called by God, think about Jesus, who was sent to us and is the high priest of our faith. ²Jesus was faithful to God as Moses was in God's family. ³Jesus has more honor than Moses, just as the builder of a house has more honor than the house itself. ⁴Every house is built by someone, but the builder of everything is God himself. ⁵Moses was faithful in God's

NKJV

¹Therefore, holy brethren, partakers of the heavenly calling, consider the Apostle and High Priest of our confession, Christ Jesus, ²who was faithful to Him who appointed Him, as Moses also was faithful in all His house. ³For this One has been counted worthy of more glory than Moses, inasmuch as He who built the house has more honor than the house. ⁴For every house is built by someone, but He who built all things

NCV

family as a servant, and he told what God would say in the future. ⁶But Christ is faithful as a Son over God's house. And we are God's house if we keep on being very sure about our great hope.

⁷So it is as the Holy Spirit says:
"Today listen to what he says.
⁸Do not be stubborn as in the past
    when you turned against God,
    when you tested God in the desert.
⁹There your ancestors tried me and tested me
    and saw the things I did for forty years.
¹⁰I was angry with them.
    I said, 'They are not loyal to me
    and have not understood my ways.'
¹I was angry and made a promise,
    'They will never enter my rest.' "

¹²So brothers and sisters, be careful that none of you has an evil, unbelieving heart that will turn you away from the living God. ¹³But encourage each other every day while it is "today." Help each other so none of you will become hardened because sin has tricked you. ¹⁴We all share in Christ if we keep till the end the sure faith we had in the beginning.

NKJV

is God. ⁵And Moses indeed was faithful in all His house as a servant, for a testimony of those things which would be spoken afterward, ⁶but Christ as a Son over His own house, whose house we are if we hold fast the confidence and the rejoicing of the hope firm to the end.

⁷Therefore, as the Holy Spirit says:

"Today, if you will hear His voice,
⁸Do not harden your hearts as in the
    rebellion,
In the day of trial in the wilderness,
⁹Where your fathers tested Me, tried Me,
    And saw My works forty years.
¹⁰Therefore I was angry with that generation,
    And said, 'They always go astray in their
        heart,
    And they have not known My ways.'
¹¹So I swore in My wrath,
    'They shall not enter My rest.' "

¹²Beware, brethren, lest there be in any of you an evil heart of unbelief in departing from the living God; ¹³but exhort one another daily, while it is called "Today," lest any of you be hardened through the deceitfulness of sin. ¹⁴For we have become partakers of Christ if we hold the beginning of our confidence steadfast to the end.

DISCOVERY

Explore the Bible reading by discussing these questions.

2. Why is Jesus worthy of greater honor than Moses?

_____

_____

_____

3. How can people demonstrate that they belong in God's house?

_____

_____

_____

4. What warning does the Holy Spirit give to us?

_____

_____

_____

5. Why do some people turn away from God?

_____

_____

_____

6. What practical advice does this passage offer us on remaining faithful to God?

_____

_____

_____

INSPIRATION

Here is an uplifting thought from the *Inspirational Study Bible.*

In reading carefully through the New Testament to see just what kind of an experience you can expect, I find that the New Testament sets forth only one. There is just one experience for which you can look—only one feeling you can expect—and that is the experience of faith. Believing is an experience as real as any experience, yet many are looking for something more—some dramatic sensation that will bring a physical thrill, while others look for some spectacular manifestation. Many have been told to look for such sensations, but the Bible says that a man is "justified by faith" and not by feeling. A man is saved by trusting in the finished work of Christ on the cross and not by physical excitement or religious ecstasy.

But you may say to me, "What about feeling? Is there no place in saving faith for any feeling?" Certainly there is room for feeling in saving faith, but we are not saved by it. Whatever feeling there may be is only the result of saving faith, but it in itself is not what does the saving! ...

Finally, someone may say, "I believe the historic facts of the gospel, but still I am not saved." Perhaps so, for the faith that saves has one distinguishing quality—saving faith is a faith that produces obedience, it is a faith that brings about a way of life. Some have quite successfully imitated this way of life for a time, but for those who trust Christ for salvation, that faith brings about in them a desire to live out that inward experience of faith. It is a power that results in godly living and surrender.

(from *Peace with God*
by Billy Graham)

RESPONSE

Use these questions to share more deeply with each other.

7. Why should believers distinguish between faith and feelings?

_____

_____

_____

8. How can you determine if your faith is real?

_____

_____

_____

9. What can you do to ensure that your faith will endure?

_____

_____

_____

PRAYER

Father, we ask you to deepen our faith in you. Give us the strength to withstand temptation, overcome doubt, and remain loyal to you. At the end of our lives, may we hear your words, "Well done, my good and faithful servant."

JOURNALING

Take a few moments to record your personal insights from this lesson.

What steps can I take this week to strengthen my faith in God?

ADDITIONAL QUESTIONS

10. How can you avoid hardening your heart against God?

_____

_____

_____

11. What is the danger for Christians who neglect the fellowship of other believers?

_____

_____

_____

12. What Christian friend can you encourage in spiritual matters? How?

_____

_____

_____

For more Bible passages about remaining faithful, see Deuteronomy 11:13–18; 1 Samuel 12:24; 2 Samuel 22:26; 1 Kings 2:3,4; 2 Chronicles 19:9; Psalm 97:10; Proverbs 28:20; Matthew 25:19–23; 1 Corinthians 4:2; 10:12, 13; 3 John 3–5; Revelation 2:10; 17:14.

To complete the book of Hebrews during this twelve-part study, read Hebrews 3:1–19.

ADDITIONAL THOUGHTS

LESSON THREE

GOD'S REST

REFLECTION

Begin your study by sharing thoughts on this question.

1. What misconceptions do people have about finding true peace?

_____

_____

_____

BIBLE READING

Read Hebrews 4:1–11 from the NCV or the NKJV.

NCV

¹Now, since God has left us the promise that we may enter his rest, let us be very careful so none of you will fail to enter. ²The Good News was preached to us just as it was to them. But the teaching they heard did not help them, because they heard it but did not accept it with faith. ³We who have believed are able to enter and have God's rest. As God has said,

NKJV

¹Therefore, since a promise remains of entering His rest, let us fear lest any of you seem to have come short of it. ²For indeed the gospel was preached to us as well as to them; but the word which they heard did not profit them, not being mixed with faith in those who heard it. ³For we who have believed do enter that rest, as He has said:

NCV

"I was angry and made a promise,
'They will never enter my rest.'"
But God's work was finished from the time he made the world. ⁴In the Scriptures he talked about the seventh day of the week: "And on the seventh day God rested from all his works." ⁵And again in the Scripture God said, "They will never enter my rest."

⁶It is still true that some people will enter God's rest, but those who first heard the way to be saved did not enter, because they did not obey. ⁷So God planned another day, called "today." He spoke about that day through David a long time later in the same Scripture used before:

"Today listen to what he says.
Do not be stubborn."

⁸We know that Joshua did not lead the people into that rest, because God spoke later about another day. ⁹This shows that the rest for God's people is still coming. ¹⁰Anyone who enters God's rest will rest from his work as God did. ¹¹Let us try as hard as we can to enter God's rest so that no one will fail by following the example of those who refused to obey.

NKJV

"So I swore in My wrath,
'They shall not enter My rest,'"
although the works were finished from the foundation of the world. ⁴For He has spoken in a certain place of the seventh day in this way: "And God rested on the seventh day from all His works"; ⁵and again in this place: "They shall not enter My rest."

⁶Since therefore it remains that some must enter it, and those to whom it was first preached did not enter because of disobedience, ⁷again He designates a certain day, saying in David, "Today," after such a long time, as it has been said:

"Today, if you will hear His voice,
Do not harden your hearts."

⁸For if Joshua had given them rest, then He would not afterward have spoken of another day. ⁹There remains therefore a rest for the people of God. ¹⁰For he who has entered His rest has himself also ceased from his works as God did from His.

¹¹Let us therefore be diligent to enter that rest, lest anyone fall according to the same example of disobedience.

DISCOVERY

Explore the Bible reading by discussing these questions.

2. Why didn't the Hebrews enter God's rest?

_____

_____

_____

3. Why won't some people be helped by the Gospel?

_____

_____

_____

4. How can people enter God's rest?

_____

_____

_____

5. How can we know that God's rest is still coming?

_____

_____

_____

6. Why should Christians avoid following the example of the Hebrew people?

_____

_____

_____

INSPIRATION

Here is an uplifting thought from the *Inspirational Study Bible.*

Sleep is determined to bring the day to a close and joy is determined to stretch the day out as long as possible. One last enchanted kingdom. One last giggle. One last game.

Maybe you are like that. Maybe, if you had your way, your day would never end. Every moment demands to be savored. You resist sleep as long as possible because you love being awake so much. If you are like that, congratulations. If not, welcome to the majority.

Most of us have learned another way of going to bed, haven't we? It's called crash and burn. Life is so full of games that the last thing we want is another one as we are trying to sleep. So, for most of us, it's good-bye world, hello pillow. Sleep, for many, is not a robber but a refuge; eight hours of relief for our wounded souls.

And if you are kept awake, it's not by counting your fingers, but by counting your debts, tasks, or even your tears.

You are tired.

You are weary.

Weary of being slapped by the waves of broken dreams.

Weary of being stepped on and run over in the endless marathon to the top.

Weary of trusting in someone only to have that trust returned in an envelope with no return address.

Weary of staring into the future and seeing only futility.

What steals our childhood zeal? …

It is this weariness that makes the words of the carpenter so compelling. Listen to them. "Come to me, all you who are weary and burdened and I will give you rest."

Come to me.… The invitation is to come to him. Why him?

He offers the invitation as a penniless rabbi in an oppressed nation. He has no connections with the authorities in Rome. He hasn't written a best-seller or earned a diploma.

Yet, he dares to look into the leathery faces of farmers and tired faces of housewives and offer rest. He looks into the disillusioned eyes of a bartender and makes this paradoxical promise: "Take my yoke upon you and learn from me, for I am gentle and humble in heart, and you will find rest for your souls."

The people came. They came out of the cul-de-sacs and office complexes of their existence and he gave them, not religion, not doctrine, not systems, but rest.

As a result, they called him Lord.

As a result, they called him Savior.

Not so much because of what he said, but because of what he did.

What he did on the cross during six hours, one Friday.

(from *Six Hours One Friday*
by Max Lucado)

RESPONSE

Use these questions to share more deeply with each other.

7. What is the rest God offers his people?

_____

_____

_____

8. How can we experience God's rest both now and in the future?

_____

_____

_____

9. What keeps us from enjoying the rest God offers?

_____

_____

_____

PRAYER

We thank you, Father, that we can experience your rest both now and for all of eternity. Teach us to appreciate and enjoy the peace you offer us today. Protect us from unbelief and disobedience so that nothing will keep us from entering your eternal rest.

JOURNALING

Take a few moments to record your personal insights from this lesson.

What steps can I take to more fully enjoy God's rest this week?

ADDITIONAL QUESTIONS

10. How is your life different since you first discovered peace with God?

_____

_____

_____

11. In what area of your life are you still not enjoying God's rest?

_____

_____

_____

12. How can you explain God's rest to a non-Christian?

_____

_____

_____

For more Bible passages about God's rest, see Exodus 31:15–17; 33:14; Psalm 16:9–11; 62:1–5; 95:10, 11; 116:7; Isaiah 11:10; Jeremiah 6:16; Matthew 11:28–30; Revelation 14:13.

To complete the book of Hebrews during this twelve-part study, read Hebrews 4:1–13.

LESSON FOUR

JESUS—OUR HIGH PRIEST

REFLECTION

Begin your study by sharing thoughts on this question.

1. Who knows your deepest secrets? Why do you trust that person?

_____

_____

_____

BIBLE READING

Read Hebrews 4:14–5:10 from the NCV or the NKJV.

NCV

¹⁴Since we have a great high priest, Jesus the Son of God, who has gone into heaven, let us hold on to the faith we have. ¹⁵For our high priest is able to understand our weaknesses. When he lived on earth, he was tempted in every way that we are, but he did not sin. ¹⁶Let us, then, feel very sure that we can come before

NKJV

¹⁴Seeing then that we have a great High Priest who has passed through the heavens, Jesus the Son of God, let us hold fast our confession. ¹⁵For we do not have a High Priest who cannot sympathize with our weaknesses, but was in all points tempted as we are, yet without sin. ¹⁶Let us therefore come boldly to the

NCV

God's throne where there is grace. There we can receive mercy and grace to help us when we need it.

Chapter 5

[1]Every high priest is chosen from among other people. He is given the work of going before God for them to offer gifts and sacrifices for sins. [2]Since he himself is weak, he is able to be gentle with those who do not understand and who are doing wrong things. [3]Because he is weak, the high priest must offer sacrifices for his own sins and also for the sins of the people.

[4]To be a high priest is an honor, but no one chooses himself for this work. He must be called by God as Aaron was. [5]So also Christ did not choose himself to have the honor of being a high priest, but God chose him. God said to him,

"You are my Son.
   Today I have become your Father."
[6]And in another Scripture God says,
"You are a priest forever,
   a priest like Melchizedek."

[7]While Jesus lived on earth, he prayed to God and asked God for help. He prayed with loud cries and tears to the One who could save him from death, and his prayer was heard because he trusted God. [8]Even though Jesus was the Son of God, he learned obedience by what he suffered. [9]And because his obedience was perfect, he was able to give eternal salvation to all who obey him. [10]In this way God made Jesus a high priest, a priest like Melchizedek.

NKJV

throne of grace, that we may obtain mercy and find grace to help in time of need.

Chapter 5

[1]For every high priest taken from among men is appointed for men in things pertaining to God, that he may offer both gifts and sacrifices for sins. [2]He can have compassion on those who are ignorant and going astray, since he himself is also subject to weakness. [3]Because of this he is required as for the people, so also for himself, to offer sacrifices for sins. [4]And no man takes this honor to himself, but he who is called by God, just as Aaron was.

[5]So also Christ did not glorify Himself to become High Priest, but it was He who said to Him:

"You are My Son,
   Today I have begotten You."

[6]As He also says in another place:

"You are a priest forever
   According to the order of Melchizedek";

[7]who, in the days of His flesh, when He had offered up prayers and supplications, with vehement cries and tears to Him who was able to save Him from death, and was heard because of His godly fear, [8]though He was a Son, yet He learned obedience by the things which He suffered. [9]And having been perfected, He became the author of eternal salvation to all who obey Him, [10]called by God as High Priest "according to the order of Melchizedek"

DISCOVERY

Explore the Bible reading by discussing these questions.

2. With what attitude should Christians approach God's throne?

_____

_____

_____

3. Describe the role and responsibilities of a high priest.

_____

_____

_____

4. What qualified Jesus to become the ultimate high priest?

_____

_____

_____

5. In what ways was Jesus similar to other high priests? How was he different?

_____

_____

_____

6. Why can Jesus offer you eternal salvation?

_____

_____

_____

INSPIRATION

Here is an uplifting thought from the *Inspirational Study Bible.*

When it comes to the major-league difficulties like death, disease, sin and disaster—you know that God cares.

But what about the smaller things? What about grouchy bosses or flat tires or lost dogs? What about broken dishes, late flights, toothaches, or a crashed hard disk? Do these matter to God?

I mean, he's got a universe to run. He's got the planets to keep balanced and presidents and kings to watch over. He's got wars to worry with and famines to fix. Who am I to tell him about my ingrown toenail?

I'm glad you asked. Let me tell you who you are. In fact, let me *proclaim* who you are.

You are an heir of God and a co-heir with Christ.

You are eternal, like an angel.

You have a crown that will last forever.

You are a holy priest, a treasured possession.

You were chosen before the creation of the world. You are destined for "praise, fame, and honor, and you will be a holy people to the Lord your God."

But more than any of the above—more significant than any title or position—is the simple fact that you are God's child. "The Father has loved us so much that we are called children of God. And we really are his children."

I love that last phrase! "We really are his children." It's as if John knew some of us would shake our heads and say, "Naw, not me. Mother Teresa, maybe. Billy Graham, all right. But not me." If those are your feelings, John added that phrase for you.

"We *really* are his children."

As a result, if something is important to you, it's important to God. . . .

So go ahead. Tell God what hurts. Talk to him. He won't turn you away. He won't think it's silly. "For our high priest is *able to understand* our weaknesses. When he lived on earth, he was tempted in every way that we are, but he did not sin. Let us, then, feel very sure that we can come before God's throne where there is grace."

Does God care about the little things in our lives? You better believe it.

If it matters to you, it matters to him.

(from *He Still Moves Stones*
by Max Lucado)

RESPONSE

Use these questions to share more deeply with each other.

7. What kind of relationship does Jesus want to have with us?

_____

_____

_____

8. When have you felt reluctant to go to Jesus with a need or concern? Why?

_____

_____

_____

9. How does it feel to carry your burdens alone? How does it feel to release them to God?

_____

_____

_____

PRAYER

Father, you know our goals and dreams for the future, our deepest hurts and disappointments, even our weaknesses and failures. You understand us completely. Teach us to be open and honest with you, not for your benefit, but for ours.

JOURNALING

Take a few moments to record your personal insights from this lesson.

What area of my life have I held back from Jesus? How can I trust him with that part of my life?

ADDITIONAL QUESTIONS

10. Why is it important to understand Jesus' role as high priest?

_____

_____

_____

11. How would your life be different if you released all of your problems to Jesus?

_____

_____

_____

12. What can you do to develop the habit of turning to God with your joys and concerns?

_____

_____

_____

For more Bible passages about Jesus' relationship with believers, see John 15:5; Romans 5:11; 1 Timothy 1:15; Hebrews 2:9–11; 6:19, 20; 7:22–26; 8:1, 2; 1 Peter 2:4–10.

To complete the book of Hebrews during this twelve-part study, read Hebrews 4:14–5:14.

ADDITIONAL THOUGHTS

LESSON FIVE

PERSEVERANCE

REFLECTION

Begin your study by sharing thoughts on this question.

1. Think of a time when you worked hard to reach a personal goal. What helped you persevere?

_____

_____

_____

BIBLE READING

Read Hebrews 6:7–20 from the NCV or the NKJV.

NCV

⁷Some people are like land that gets plenty of rain. The land produces a good crop for those who work it, and it receives God's blessings. ⁸Other people are like land that grows thorns and weeds and is worthless. It is in danger of being cursed by God and will be destroyed by fire.

⁹Dear friends, we are saying this to you, but we really expect better things from you that will

NKJV

⁷For the earth which drinks in the rain that often comes upon it, and bears herbs useful for those by whom it is cultivated, receives blessing from God; ⁸but if it bears thorns and briars, it is rejected and near to being cursed, whose end is to be burned.

⁹But, beloved, we are confident of better things concerning you, yes, things that accompany salvation, though we speak in this

NCV

lead to your salvation. [10]God is fair; he will not forget the work you did and the love you showed for him by helping his people. And he will remember that you are still helping them. [11]We want each of you to go on with the same hard work all your lives so you will surely get what you hope for. [12]We do not want you to become lazy. Be like those who through faith and patience will receive what God has promised.

[13]God made a promise to Abraham. And as there is no one greater than God, he used himself when he swore to Abraham, [14]saying, "I will surely bless you and give you many descendants." [15]Abraham waited patiently for this to happen, and he received what God promised.

[16]People always use the name of someone greater than themselves when they swear. The oath proves that what they say is true, and this ends all arguing. [17]God wanted to prove that his promise was true to those who would get what he promised. And he wanted them to understand clearly that his purposes never change, so he made an oath. [18]These two things cannot change: God cannot lie when he makes a promise, and he cannot lie when he makes an oath. These things encourage us who came to God for safety. They give us strength to hold on to the hope we have been given. [19]We have this hope as an anchor for the soul, sure and strong. It enters behind the curtain in the Most Holy Place in heaven, [20]where Jesus has gone ahead of us and for us. He has become the high priest forever, a priest like Melchizedek.

NKJV

manner. [10]For God is not unjust to forget your work and labor of love which you have shown toward His name, in that you have ministered to the saints, and do minister. [11]And we desire that each one of you show the same diligence to the full assurance of hope until the end, [12]that you do not become sluggish, but imitate those who through faith and patience inherit the promises.

[13]For when God made a promise to Abraham, because He could swear by no one greater, He swore by Himself, [14]saying, "Surely blessing I will bless you, and multiplying I will multiply you." [15]And so, after he had patiently endured, he obtained the promise. [16]For men indeed swear by the greater, and an oath for confirmation is for them an end of all dispute. [17]Thus God, determining to show more abundantly to the heirs of promise the immutability of His counsel, confirmed it by an oath, [18]that by two immutable things, in which it is impossible for God to lie, we might have strong consolation, who have fled for refuge to lay hold of the hope set before us.

[19]This hope we have as an anchor of the soul, both sure and steadfast, and which enters the Presence behind the veil, [20]where the forerunner has entered for us, even Jesus, having become High Priest forever according to the order of Melchizedek.

DISCOVERY

Explore the Bible reading by discussing these questions.

2. Whom does God bless? Whom does he curse?

_____

_____

_____

3. How does God demonstrate his fairness to his people?

_____

_____

_____

4. What promise has God given us? How do we know that the promise is secure?

_____

_____

_____

5. Why is it encouraging to know that God's purposes never change?

_____

_____

_____

6. God cannot lie. What kind of security does that give you?

_____

_____

_____

INSPIRATION

Here is an uplifting thought from the *Inspirational Study Bible.*

In the barren prairie, the hiker huddles down. The cold northerly sweeps over him, stinging his face and numbing his fingers. The whistle of the wind is deafening. The hiker hugs his knees to his chest, yearning for warmth.

He doesn't move. The sky is orange with dirt. His teeth are grainy, his eyes sooty. He thinks of quitting. Going home. Home to the mountains.

"Ahh. The mountains." The spirit that moved him in the mountains seems so far away. For a moment, his mind wanders back to his homeland. Green country. Mountain trails. Fresh water. Hikers hiking on well marked trails. No surprises, few fears, rich companionship.

One day, while on a brisk hike, he had stopped to look out from the mountains across the neighboring desert. He felt strangely pulled to the sweeping barrenness that lay before him. The next day he paused again. And the next, and the next. "Shouldn't someone try to take life to the desert?" Slowly the flicker in his heart became a flame.

Many agreed that someone should go, but no one volunteered.

Uncharted land, fearful storms, loneliness.

But the hiker, spurred by the enthusiasm of others, determined to go. After careful preparation, he set out, alone. With the cheers of his friends behind him, he descended the grassy highlands and entered the desolate wilderness.

The first few days his steps were springy and his eye was keen. He yearned to do his part to bring life to the desert. Then came the heat. The scorpions. The monotony. The snakes. Slowly, the fire diminished. And now . . . the storm. The endless roar of the wind. The relentless, cursed cold.

"I don't know how much more I can take." Weary and beaten, the hiker considers going back. "At least I got this far." Knees tucked under him, head bowed, almost touching the ground. "Will it ever stop?"

Grimly he laughs at the irony of the situation. "Some hiker. Too tired to go on, yet too ashamed to go home." Deep, deep is the struggle. No longer can he hear the voices of friends. Long gone is the romance of his mission. No longer does he float on the fancifulness of a dream.

"Maybe someone else should do this. I'm too young, too inexperienced." The winds of discouragement and fear whip at his fire, exhausting what is left of the flame. But the coals remain, hidden and hot.

The hiker, now almost the storm's victim, looks one last time for the fire. (Is there any greater challenge than of stirring a spirit while in the clutches of defeat?) Yearning and clawing, the temptation to quit is gradually overcome by the urge to go on. Blowing on the coals, the hiker once again hears the call to the desert. Though faint, the call is clear.

With all the strength he can summon, the hiker rises to his feet, bows his head, and takes his first step into the wind.

(from *On the Anvil*
by Max Lucado)

RESPONSE

Use these questions to share more deeply with each other.

7. What is a Christian's primary goal in this life?

_____

_____

_____

8. What obstacles stand in the way of your fulfilling this goal?

_____

_____

_____

9. How can we prepare ourselves to face and overcome those obstacles?

_____ _____

_____

_____

PRAYER

Father, help us to maintain our promise of faithfulness to you, even in times when we are filled with doubt, fear, and insecurity. Give us great courage to endure the storms that come our way. Help us press on toward the goal you have set for us.

JOURNALING

Take a few moments to record your personal insights from this lesson.

What fears and doubts do I face today? How does this passage challenge me to deal with those feelings?

ADDITIONAL QUESTIONS

10. What does it mean to trust God's promises?

_____

_____

_____

11. What are the rewards of trusting God?

_____

_____

_____

12. Which of God's promises will you remember this week to help you persevere?

_____

_____

_____

For more Bible passages about perseverance, see Acts 20:24; Romans 5:3, 4;
1 Timothy 4:16; 2 Timothy 2:12; Hebrews 10:36; 12:1–3; James 1:2–4, 12; 5:11;
2 Peter 1:5–11; Revelation 2:2, 3.

To complete the book of Hebrews during this twelve-part study, read
Hebrews 6:1–7:28.

LESSON SIX

GOD FORGIVES AND FORGETS

REFLECTION

Begin your study by sharing thoughts on this question.

1. Think of a time when you received forgiveness from a friend. How did it make you feel?

_____ -

_____

_____ ... ..

BIBLE READING

Read Hebrews 8:1–13 from the NCV or the NKJV.

NCV

¹Here is the point of what we are saying: We have a high priest who sits on the right side of God's throne in heaven. ²Our high priest serves in the Most Holy Place, the true place of worship that was made by God, not by humans.

³Every high priest has the work of offering gifts and sacrifices to God. So our high priest

NKJV

¹Now this is the main point of the things we are saying: We have such a High Priest, who is seated at the right hand of the throne of the Majesty in the heavens, ²a Minister of the sanctuary and of the true tabernacle which the Lord erected, and not man.

³For every high priest is appointed to offer

NCV

must also offer something to God. ⁴If our high priest were now living on earth, he would not be a priest, because there are already priests here who follow the law by offering gifts to God. ⁵The work they do as priests is only a copy and a shadow of what is in heaven. This is why God warned Moses when he was ready to build the Holy Tent:"Be very careful to make everything by the plan I showed you on the mountain." ⁶But the priestly work that has been given to Jesus is much greater than the work that was given to the other priests. In the same way, the new agreement that Jesus brought from God to his people is much greater than the old one. And the new agreement is based on promises of better things.

⁷If there had been nothing wrong with the first agreement, there would have been no need for a second agreement. ⁸But God found something wrong with his people. He says:

"Look, the time is coming, says the Lord,
    when I will make a new agreement
with the people of Israel
    and the people of Judah.
⁹It will not be1 like the agreement
    I made with their ancestors
when I took them by the hand
    to bring them out of Egypt.
But they broke that agreement,
    and I turned away from them, says the
        Lord.
¹⁰This is the agreement I will make
    with the people of Israel at that time,
        says the Lord.
I will put my teachings in their minds and
    write them on their hearts.

NKJV

both gifts and sacrifices. Therefore it is necessary that this One also have something to offer. ⁴For if He were on earth, He would not be a priest, since there are priests who offer the gifts according to the law; ⁵who serve the copy and shadow of the heavenly things, as Moses was divinely instructed when he was about to make the tabernacle. For He said,"See that you make all things according to the pattern shown you on the mountain." ⁶But now He has obtained a more excellent ministry, inasmuch as He is also Mediator of a better covenant, which was established on better promises.

⁷For if that first covenant had been faultless, then no place would have been sought for a second. ⁸Because finding fault with them, He says: "Behold, the days are coming, says the LORD, when I will make a new covenant with the house of Israel and with the house of Judah— ⁹not according to the covenant that I made with their fathers in the day when I took them by the hand to lead them out of the land of Egypt; because they did not continue in My covenant, and I disregarded them, says the LORD. ¹⁰For this is the covenant that I will make with the house of Israel after those days, says the LORD: I will put My laws in their mind and write them on their hearts; and I will be their God, and they shall be My people. ¹¹None of them shall teach his neighbor, and none his brother, saying,'Know the LORD,' for all shall know Me, from the least of them to the greatest of them. ¹²For I will be merciful to their unrighteousness, and their sins and their lawless deeds I will remember no more."

NCV

I will be their God,
    and they will be my people.
¹¹People will no longer have to teach their
        neighbors and relatives
    to know the Lord,
because all people will know me,
    from the least to the most important.
¹²I will forgive them for the wicked things
        they did,
    and I will not remember their sins
        anymore."
¹³God called this a new agreement, so he has
made the first agreement old. And anything
that is old and worn out is ready to disappear.

NKJV

¹³In that He says, "A new covenant," He has
made the first obsolete. Now what is becoming
obsolete and growing old is ready to vanish
away.

DISCOVERY

Explore the Bible reading by discussing these questions.

2. How does Jesus fulfill his duties as high priest?

_____

_____

_____

3. Why is Jesus' priestly work greater than the work of other priests?

_____

_____

_____

4. How is the new covenant different from the old covenant?

_____

_____

_____

5. Why did God establish a new agreement with his people?

_____

_____

_____

6. What promises did God make to his people?

_____

_____

_____

INSPIRATION

Here is an uplifting thought from the *Inspirational Study Bible*.

I was thanking the Father today for his mercy. I began listing the sins he'd forgiven. One by one I thanked God for forgiving my stumbles and tumbles. My motives were pure and my heart was thankful, but my understanding of God was wrong. It was when I used the word "remember" that it hit me. . . .

God doesn't just forgive, he forgets. He erases the board. He destroys the evidence. He burns the microfilm. He clears the computer. . . .

No, he doesn't remember. But I do, you do. You still remember. You're like me. You still remember what you did before you changed. In the cellar of your heart lurk the ghosts of yesterday's sins. Sins you've confessed; errors of which you've repented; damage you've done your best to repair.

And though you're a different person, the ghosts still linger. Though you've locked the basement door, they still haunt you. They float to meet you, spooking your soul and robbing your joy. With wordless whispers they remind you of moments when you forgot whose child you were. . . .

Poltergeists from yesterday's pitfalls. Spiteful specters that slyly suggest, "Are you really forgiven? Sure God forgets most of our mistakes, but do you think he could actually forget the time you . . ."

Was [God] exaggerating when he said he would cast our sins as far as the east is from the west? Do you actually believe he would make a statement like "I will not hold their iniquities against them" and then rub our noses in them whenever we ask for help? . . .

You see, God is either the God of perfect grace . . . or he is not God. Grace forgets. Period. He who is perfect love cannot hold grudges. If he does, then he isn't perfect love. And if he isn't perfect love, you might as well put this book down and go fishing, because both of us are chasing fairy tales.

But I believe in his loving forgetfulness. And I believe he has a graciously terrible memory.

(from *God Came Near*
by Max Lucado)

RESPONSE

Use these questions to share more deeply with each other.

7. What do you usually expect when you ask a friend for forgiveness?

_____

_____

_____

8. What can we expect from God when we confess our sins to him?

_____

_____

_____

9. How can you remind yourself that God has forgiven you and does not hold your sin against you?

_____

_____

_____

PRAYER

Thank you, Father, for your forgiveness and your gracious forgetfulness. Teach us to confess our sins quickly, to fully accept your forgiveness so that we can enjoy a restored relationship with you, and to release any feelings of guilt or self-condemnation. May we experience the joy and freedom your forgiveness brings.

JOURNALING

Take a few moments to record your personal insights from this lesson.

What past sins haunt me? How can I learn to forgive myself for the sins God has already forgiven?

ADDITIONAL QUESTIONS

10. Why do we sometimes doubt God's forgiveness?

_____

_____

_____

11. How can we find freedom from a false sense of guilt?

_____

_____

_____

12. Why is it important for believers to express thanks to God for his forgiveness?

_____

_____

_____

For more Bible passages about God's forgiveness, see Numbers 14:18–20; 2 Chronicles 7:14; Nehemiah 9:17; Psalm 86:5; 103:3; Daniel 9:9; Micah 7:18; Matthew 6:12–14; Mark 2:5–12; Colossians 2:13, 14; 3:13; 1 John 1:9.

To complete the book of Hebrews during this twelve-part study, read Hebrews 8:1–13.

LESSON SEVEN

A SACRIFICE FOR SINS

REFLECTION

Begin your study by sharing thoughts on this question.

1. How often do you think about Christ's death on the cross? What does his suffering for you make you feel?

_____

_____

_____

BIBLE READING

Read Hebrews 9:11–28 from the NCV or the NKJV.

NCV

¹¹But when Christ came as the high priest of the good things we now have, he entered the greater and more perfect tent. It is not made by humans and does not belong to this world. ¹²Christ entered the Most Holy Place only once—and for all time. He did not take with him the blood of goats and calves. His sacrifice was his own blood, and by it he set us free from sin forever. ¹³The blood of goats and bulls and

NKJV

¹¹But Christ came as High Priest of the good things to come, with the greater and more perfect tabernacle not made with hands, that is, not of this creation. ¹²Not with the blood of goats and calves, but with His own blood He entered the Most Holy Place once for all, having obtained eternal redemption. ¹³For if the blood of bulls and goats and the ashes of a heifer, sprinkling the unclean, sanctifies for the

NCV

the ashes of a cow are sprinkled on the people who are unclean, and this makes their bodies clean again. [14]How much more is done by the blood of Christ. He offered himself through the eternal Spirit as a perfect sacrifice to God. His blood will make our consciences pure from useless acts so we may serve the living God.

[15]For this reason Christ brings a new agreement from God to his people. Those who are called by God can now receive the blessings he has promised, blessings that will last forever. They can have those things because Christ died so that the people who lived under the first agreement could be set free from sin.

[16]When there is a will, it must be proven that the one who wrote that will is dead. [17]A will means nothing while the person is alive; it can be used only after the person dies. [18]This is why even the first agreement could not begin without blood to show death. [19]First, Moses told all the people every command in the law. Next he took the blood of calves and mixed it with water. Then he used red wool and a branch of the hyssop plant to sprinkle it on the book of the law and on all the people. [20]He said, "This is the blood that begins the Agreement that God commanded you to obey." [21]In the same way, Moses sprinkled the blood on the Holy Tent and over all the things used in worship. [22]The law says that almost everything must be made clean by blood, and sins cannot be forgiven without blood to show death.

[23]So the copies of the real things in heaven had to be made clean by animal sacrifices. But the real things in heaven need much better sacrifices. [24]Christ did not go into the Most Holy

NKJV

purifying of the flesh, [14]how much more shall the blood of Christ, who through the eternal Spirit offered Himself without spot to God, cleanse your conscience from dead works to serve the living God? [15]And for this reason He is the Mediator of the new covenant, by means of death, for the redemption of the transgressions under the first covenant, that those who are called may receive the promise of the eternal inheritance.

[16]For where there is a testament, there must also of necessity be the death of the testator. [17]For a testament is in force after men are dead, since it has no power at all while the testator lives. [18]Therefore not even the first covenant was dedicated without blood. [19]For when Moses had spoken every precept to all the people according to the law, he took the blood of calves and goats, with water, scarlet wool, and hyssop, and sprinkled both the book itself and all the people, [20]saying, "This is the blood of the covenant which God has commanded you." [21]Then likewise he sprinkled with blood both the tabernacle and all the vessels of the ministry. [22]And according to the law almost all things are purified with blood, and without shedding of blood there is no remission.

[23]Therefore it was necessary that the copies of the things in the heavens should be purified with these, but the heavenly things themselves with better sacrifices than these. [24]For Christ has not entered the holy places made with hands, which are copies of the true, but into heaven itself, now to appear in the presence of God for us; [25]not that He should offer Himself often, as the high priest enters the Most Holy

NCV

Place made by humans, which is only a copy of the real one. He went into heaven itself and is there now before God to help us. ²⁵The high priest enters the Most Holy Place once every year with blood that is not his own. But Christ did not offer himself many times. ²⁶Then he would have had to suffer many times since the world was made. But Christ came only once and for all time at just the right time to take away all sin by sacrificing himself. ²⁷Just as everyone must die once and be judged, ²⁸so Christ was offered as a sacrifice one time to take away the sins of many people. And he will come a second time, not to offer himself for sin, but to bring salvation to those who are waiting for him.

NKJV

Place every year with blood of another— ²⁶He then would have had to suffer often since the foundation of the world; but now, once at the end of the ages, He has appeared to put away sin by the sacrifice of Himself. ²⁷And as it is appointed for men to die once, but after this the judgment, ²⁸so Christ was offered once to bear the sins of many. To those who eagerly wait for Him He will appear a second time, apart from sin, for salvation.

DISCOVERY

Explore the Bible reading by discussing these questions.

2. How can people receive the blessings God has promised?

_____

_____

_____

3. Why did Christ establish a new agreement between God and people?

_____

_____

_____

4. Why is the shedding of blood necessary for the forgiveness of sins?

_____

_____

_____

5. How does Christ's blood purify us?

_____

_____

_____

6. How was Christ's sacrifice superior to the sacrifice of animals?

_____

_____

_____

INSPIRATION

Here is an uplifting thought from the *Inspirational Study Bible*.

Sin incurs the death penalty and no man has the ability in himself to save himself from its penalty or to cleanse his own heart of its corruption. . . .

Man's only salvation from sin stands on a lonely, barren, skull-shaped hill; a thief hangs on one cross, a murderer on another and between them, a Man with a crown of thorns. Blood flows from His hands and feet, it pours from His side, it drops down his face—while those who stand looking on sneer and mock him.

And who is this tortured figure, who is this Man whom other men seek to humiliate and kill? He is the Son of God, the Prince of Peace, heaven's own appointed Messenger to the sin-ridden earth. This is He, before whom angels fall down and veil their faces. And yet He hangs bleeding and forsaken upon the cross.

What brought Him to this place of horrors? Who inflicted that hideous torture upon the Man who came to teach us love? You did and I did, for it was for your sin and my sin that Jesus was nailed to the cross. In this immortal moment the human race experienced the darkest reaches of sin, it sank to its lowest depths, it touched its foulest limits. No wonder that the sun could not endure and veiled its face! . . .

But sin overreached itself on the cross. Man's hideous injustice that crucified Christ became the means that opened the way for man to become free. Sin's masterpiece of shame and hate became God's masterpiece of mercy and forgiveness.

(from *Peace with God*
by Billy Graham)

RESPONSE

Use these questions to share more deeply with each other.

7. How do people try to make themselves right with God? What results from their efforts?

_____

_____

_____

8. What can free us from the frustration of trying to earn God's approval?

_____

_____

_____

9. What is significant about the fact that Christ died "once for all"?

_____

_____

_____

PRAYER

Because of your great love for us, Father, you sacrificed your only Son so that we could receive forgiveness for our sins and enjoy eternal life with you. We are thankful that you did not hold anything back in your plan to save us. Show us how to give ourselves completely to you in return.

JOURNALING

Take a few moments to record your personal insights from this lesson.

What benefits and blessings do I enjoy because of Jesus' death on the cross?

ADDITIONAL QUESTIONS

10. How would you explain to an unbelieving friend why Jesus had to die?

_____

_____

_____

11. How would your life be different if Christ had not died?

_____

_____

_____

12. How can you thank Jesus today for sacrificing his life to save you?

_____

_____

_____

For more Bible passages about Christ's sacrifice for sin, see John 1:29; Romans 3:22–27; 4:25; 6:23; 2 Corinthians 5:21; 2 Timothy 1:8–10; Hebrews 2:17; 7:27; 10:5–14; 1 John 1:7; 2:2; 4:10.

To complete the book of Hebrews during this twelve-part study, read Hebrews 9:1–28.

LESSON EIGHT

CONFIDENCE IN CHRIST

REFLECTION

Begin your study by sharing thoughts on this question.

1. Think of a time when God gave you courage or boldness. How did this affect your life?

_____

_____

_____

BIBLE READING

Read Hebrews 10:19–39 from the NCV or the NKJV.

NCV

¹⁹So, brothers and sisters, we are completely free to enter the Most Holy Place without fear because of the blood of Jesus' death. ²⁰We can enter through a new and living way that Jesus opened for us. It leads through the curtain—Christ's body. ²¹And since we have a great priest over God's house, ²²let us come near to God with a sincere heart and a sure faith, because we have been made free from a guilty

NKJV

¹⁹Therefore, brethren, having boldness to enter the Holiest by the blood of Jesus, ²⁰by a new and living way which He consecrated for us, through the veil, that is, His flesh, ²¹and having a High Priest over the house of God, ²²let us draw near with a true heart in full assurance of faith, having our hearts sprinkled from an evil conscience and our bodies washed with pure water. ²³Let us hold fast the confession of

NCV

conscience, and our bodies have been washed with pure water. ²³Let us hold firmly to the hope that we have confessed, because we can trust God to do what he promised.

²⁴Let us think about each other and help each other to show love and do good deeds. ²⁵You should not stay away from the church meetings, as some are doing, but you should meet together and encourage each other. Do this even more as you see the day coming.

²⁶If we decide to go on sinning after we have learned the truth, there is no longer any sacrifice for sins. ²⁷There is nothing but fear in waiting for the judgment and the terrible fire that will destroy all those who live against God. ²⁸Anyone who refused to obey the law of Moses was found guilty from the proof given by two or three witnesses. He was put to death without mercy. ²⁹So what do you think should be done to those who do not respect the Son of God, who look at the blood of the agreement that made them holy as no different from others' blood, who insult the Spirit of God's grace? Surely they should have a much worse punishment. ³⁰We know that God said, "I will punish those who do wrong; I will repay them." And he also said, "The Lord will judge his people." ³¹It is a terrible thing to fall into the hands of the living God.

³²Remember those days in the past when you first learned the truth. You had a hard struggle with many sufferings, but you continued strong. ³³Sometimes you were hurt and attacked before crowds of people, and sometimes you shared with those who were being treated that way. ³⁴You helped the prisoners. You

NKJV

our hope without wavering, for He who promised is faithful. ²⁴And let us consider one another in order to stir up love and good works, ²⁵not forsaking the assembling of ourselves together, as is the manner of some, but exhorting one another, and so much the more as you see the Day approaching.

²⁶For if we sin willfully after we have received the knowledge of the truth, there no longer remains a sacrifice for sins, ²⁷but a certain fearful expectation of judgment, and fiery indignation which will devour the adversaries. ²⁸Anyone who has rejected Moses' law dies without mercy on the testimony of two or three witnesses. ²⁹Of how much worse punishment, do you suppose, will he be thought worthy who has trampled the Son of God underfoot, counted the blood of the covenant by which he was sanctified a common thing, and insulted the Spirit of grace? ³⁰For we know Him who said, "Vengeance is Mine, I will repay," says the Lord. And again, "The LORD will judge His people." ³¹It is a fearful thing to fall into the hands of the living God.

³²But recall the former days in which, after you were illuminated, you endured a great struggle with sufferings: ³³partly while you were made a spectacle both by reproaches and tribulations, and partly while you became companions of those who were so treated; ³⁴for you had compassion on me in my chains, and joyfully accepted the plundering of your goods, knowing that you have a better and an enduring possession for yourselves in heaven. ³⁵Therefore do not cast away your confidence, which has great reward. ³⁶For you have need of

NCV

even had joy when all that you owned was taken from you, because you knew you had something better and more lasting.

³⁵So do not lose the courage you had in the past, which has a great reward. ³⁶You must hold on, so you can do what God wants and receive what he has promised. ³⁷For in a very short time,

"The One who is coming will come
  and will not be delayed.
³⁸The person who is right with me
  will live by trusting in me.
But if he turns back with fear,
  I will not be pleased with him."
³⁹But we are not those who turn back and are lost. We are people who have faith and are saved.

NKJV

endurance, so that after you have done the will of God, you may receive the promise:

³⁷"For yet a little while,
  And He who is coming will come and will
    not tarry.
³⁸Now the just shall live by faith;
  But if anyone draws back,
  My soul has no pleasure in him."

³⁹But we are not of those who draw back to perdition, but of those who believe to the saving of the soul.

DISCOVERY

Explore the Bible reading by discussing these questions.

2. What gives believers confidence to approach a holy God?

_____

_____

_____

3. List some of the opportunities and privileges Christ's death provides you.

_____

_____

_____

4. What happens when people reject God's salvation?

_____

_____

_____

5. What warnings does this passage give to people who turn away from their faith in Jesus?

_____

_____

_____

6. The author of Hebrews said that it is a terrible thing to fall into the hands of the living God. What did he mean?

_____

_____

_____

INSPIRATION

Here is an uplifting thought from the *Inspirational Study Bible*.

Picture it this way. Imagine that you are an ice skater in competition. You are in first place with one more round to go. If you perform well, the trophy is yours. You are nervous, anxious, and frightened.

Then, only minutes before your performance, your trainer rushes to you with the thrilling news: "You've already won! The judges tabulated the scores, and the person in second place can't catch you. You are too far ahead."

Upon hearing that news, how will you feel? Exhilarated!

And how will you skate? Timidly? Cautiously? Of course not. How about courageously and confidently? You bet you will. You will do your best because the prize is yours. You will skate like a champion because that is what you are! You will hear the applause of victory. . . .

The point is clear: the truth will triumph. The father of truth will win, and the followers of truth will be saved.

(from *The Applause of Heaven* by Max Lucado)

RESPONSE

Use these questions to share more deeply with each other.

7. How does Jesus' victory over death encourage you?

_____

_____

_____

8. How should our confidence in Christ's ultimate victory change the way we live?

_____

_____

_____

9. How can believers help each other to show love and do good deeds?

_____

_____

_____

PRAYER

Father, rekindle the fire that burned bright in our hearts when we first discovered your love and forgiveness. Renew our commitment to you and your work. Help us to be busy about the right business—the business of serving you.

JOURNALING

Take a few moments to record your personal insights from this lesson.

Have I lost the enthusiasm and commitment I had when I first became a Christian? How can I renew my commitment?

ADDITIONAL QUESTIONS

10. What can we gain from remembering the days when we were new believers?

_____

_____   _____

_____

11. Who is someone you can encourage to persevere through difficult times? What can you do for that person?

_____

_____

_____

12. How can you depend more on other believers to help you grow in your faith and commitment to God?

_____

_____

_____

For more Bible passages about Christ's victory over death, see John 16:33; 1 Corinthians 15:24–26, 54–58; 1 John 5:4; Revelation 3:21; 17:14.

To complete the book of Hebrews during this twelve-part study, read Hebrews 10:1–39.

LESSON NINE

FAITH IN GOD'S PROMISES

REFLECTION

Begin your study by sharing thoughts on this question.

1. Think of a time when you have been inspired by another person's faith in God. What was it that encouraged you?

_____

_____

_____

BIBLE READING

Read Hebrews 11:1–16 from the NCV or the NKJV.

NCV

¹Faith means being sure of the things we hope for and knowing that something is real even if we do not see it. ²Faith is the reason we remember great people who lived in the past.

³It is by faith we understand that the whole world was made by God's command so what we see was made by something that cannot be seen.

⁴It was by faith that Abel offered God a

NKJV

¹Now faith is the substance of things hoped for, the evidence of things not seen. ²For by it the elders obtained a good testimony.

³By faith we understand that the worlds were framed by the word of God, so that the things which are seen were not made of things which are visible.

⁴By faith Abel offered to God a more excellent sacrifice than Cain, through which he

NCV

better sacrifice than Cain did. God said he was pleased with the gifts Abel offered and called Abel a good man because of his faith. Abel died, but through his faith he is still speaking.

⁵It was by faith that Enoch was taken to heaven so he would not die. He could not be found, because God had taken him away. Before he was taken, the Scripture says that he was a man who truly pleased God. ⁶Without faith no one can please God. Anyone who comes to God must believe that he is real and that he rewards those who truly want to find him.

⁷It was by faith that Noah heard God's warnings about things he could not yet see. He obeyed God and built a large boat to save his family. By his faith, Noah showed that the world was wrong, and he became one of those who are made right with God through faith.

⁸It was by faith Abraham obeyed God's call to go to another place God promised to give him. He left his own country, not knowing where he was to go. ⁹It was by faith that he lived like a foreigner in the country God promised to give him. He lived in tents with Isaac and Jacob, who had received that same promise from God. ¹⁰Abraham was waiting for the city that has real foundations—the city planned and built by God.

¹¹He was too old to have children, and Sarah could not have children. It was by faith that Abraham was made able to become a father, because he trusted God to do what he had promised. ¹²This man was so old he was almost dead, but from him came as many descendants as there are stars in the sky. Like the sand on the seashore, they could not be counted.

NKJV

obtained witness that he was righteous, God testifying of his gifts; and through it he being dead still speaks.

⁵By faith Enoch was taken away so that he did not see death, "and was not found, because God had taken him"; for before he was taken he had this testimony, that he pleased God. ⁶But without faith it is impossible to please Him, for he who comes to God must believe that He is, and that He is a rewarder of those who diligently seek Him.

⁷By faith Noah, being divinely warned of things not yet seen, moved with godly fear, prepared an ark for the saving of his household, by which he condemned the world and became heir of the righteousness which is according to faith.

⁸By faith Abraham obeyed when he was called to go out to the place which he would receive as an inheritance. And he went out, not knowing where he was going. ⁹By faith he dwelt in the land of promise as in a foreign country, dwelling in tents with Isaac and Jacob, the heirs with him of the same promise; ¹⁰for he waited for the city which has foundations, whose builder and maker is God.

¹¹By faith Sarah herself also received strength to conceive seed, and she bore a child when she was past the age, because she judged Him faithful who had promised. ¹²Therefore from one man, and him as good as dead, were born as many as the stars of the sky in multitude—innumerable as the sand which is by the seashore.

¹³These all died in faith, not having received the promises, but having seen them afar off

NCV

¹³All these great people died in faith. They did not get the things that God promised his people, but they saw them coming far in the future and were glad. They said they were like visitors and strangers on earth. ¹⁴When people say such things, they show they are looking for a country that will be their own. ¹⁵If they had been thinking about the country they had left, they could have gone back. ¹⁶But they were waiting for a better country—a heavenly country. So God is not ashamed to be called their God, because he has prepared a city for them.

NKJV

were assured of them, embraced them and confessed that they were strangers and pilgrims on the earth. ¹⁴For those who say such things declare plainly that they seek a homeland. ¹⁵And truly if they had called to mind that country from which they had come out, they would have had opportunity to return. ¹⁶But now they desire a better, that is, a heavenly country. Therefore God is not ashamed to be called their God, for He has prepared a city for them.

DISCOVERY

Explore the Bible reading by discussing these questions.

2. Why should we remember people of faith who lived in the past?

_____

_____

_____

3. What made the faith of these people extraordinary?

_____

_____

_____

4. How did these people demonstrate their faith in God?

_____

_____

_____

5. Why did these people say they were like visitors and strangers on earth?

_____

_____

_____

6. How can God's people show their trust in his promises?

_____

_____

_____

INSPIRATION

Here is an uplifting thought from the *Inspirational Study Bible.*

Faith is the belief that God is real and that God is good. Faith is not a mystical experience or a midnight vision or a voice in the forest. . . . It is a choice to believe that the one who made it all hasn't left it all and that he still sends light into the shadows and responds to gestures of faith. . . .

Faith is not the belief that God will do what you want. Faith is the belief that God will do what is right.

"Blessed are the dirt-poor, nothing-to-give, trapped-in-a-corner, destitute, diseased," Jesus said, "for theirs is the kingdom of heaven" (Matt. 5:6, my translation).

God's economy is upside down (or rightside up and ours is upside down!). God says that the more hopeless your circumstances, the more likely your salvation. The greater your cares, the more genuine your prayers. The darker the room, the greater the need for light. . . .

God's help is near and always available, but it is only given to those who seek it. Nothing results from apathy. . . .

Compared to God's part, our part is minuscule but necessary. We don't have to do much, but we do have to do something. Write a letter. Ask forgiveness. Call a counselor. Confess. Call Mom. Visit a doctor. Be baptized. Feed a hungry person. Pray. Teach. Go.

Do something that demonstrates faith. For faith with no effort is no faith at all. God will respond. He has never rejected a genuine gesture of faith. Never.

(from *He Still Moves Stones* by Max Lucado)

RESPONSE

Use these questions to share more deeply with each other.

7. Why is it impossible to please God without faith?

_____

_____

_____

8. How do faith and obedience work together?

_____

_____

_____

9. How does God respond to our faith?

_____

_____

_____

PRAYER

Father, our faith is so weak. Forgive us for doubting you. Help us to persevere even when we haven't seen all of your promises fulfilled. Remind us that we are just passing through this life by focusing our eyes on a better country—our heavenly home.

JOURNALING

Take a few moments to record your personal insights from this lesson.

What specific things have happened in my life that remind me of God's faithfulness?

ADDITIONAL QUESTIONS

10. What encouragement does this passage offer to people who have not had their prayers answered?

_____

_____

_____

11. How has your faith in God changed your perspective or goals in life?

_____

_____

_____

12. What can you do to exercise faith this week?

_____

_____

_____

For more Bible passages about faith, see 2 Chronicles 20:20; Isaiah 7:9; Matthew 21:21, 22; John 8:30; Acts 15:8, 9; Romans 1:17; 5:1, 2; 1 Corinthians 16:13; Galatians 2:15, 16; 3:22–27; Hebrews 4:14; 10:38; James 2:14–26; 1 Peter 1:8–9; Jude 3, 20.

To complete the book of Hebrews during this twelve-part study, read Hebrews 11:1–40.

LESSON TEN

SUFFERING SERVES A PURPOSE

REFLECTION

Begin your study by sharing thoughts on this question.

1. Think of a time when you endured something painful because you knew it would ultimately benefit you. What was your experience and how did you benefit?

_____

_____

_____

BIBLE READING

Read Hebrews 12:1–11 from the NCV or the NKJV.

NCV

¹We have around us many people whose lives tell us what faith means. So let us run the race that is before us and never give up. We should remove from our lives anything that would get in the way and the sin that so easily holds us back. ²Let us look only to Jesus, the One who began our faith and who makes it perfect. He suffered death on the cross. But he accepted the shame as if it were nothing

NKJV

¹Therefore we also, since we are surrounded by so great a cloud of witnesses, let us lay aside every weight, and the sin which so easily ensnares us, and let us run with endurance the race that is set before us, ²looking unto Jesus, the author and finisher of our faith, who for the joy that was set before Him endured the cross, despising the shame, and has sat down at the right hand of the throne of God.

NCV

because of the joy that God put before him. And now he is sitting at the right side of God's throne. [3]Think about Jesus' example. He held on while wicked people were doing evil things to him. So do not get tired and stop trying.

[4]You are struggling against sin, but your struggles have not yet caused you to be killed. [5]You have forgotten the encouraging words that call you his children:

"My child, don't think the Lord's discipline
    is worth nothing,
  and don't stop trying when he corrects
    you.
[6]The Lord disciplines those he loves,
  and he punishes everyone he accepts as
    his child."

[7]So hold on through your sufferings, because they are like a father's discipline. God is treating you as children. All children are disciplined by their fathers. [8]If you are never disciplined (and every child must be disciplined), you are not true children. [9]We have all had fathers here on earth who disciplined us, and we respected them. So it is even more important that we accept discipline from the Father of our spirits so we will have life. [10]Our fathers on earth disciplined us for a short time in the way they thought was best. But God disciplines us to help us, so we can become holy as he is. [11]We do not enjoy being disciplined. It is painful, but later, after we have learned from it, we have peace, because we start living in the right way.

NKJV

[3]For consider Him who endured such hostility from sinners against Himself, lest you become weary and discouraged in your souls. [4]You have not yet resisted to bloodshed, striving against sin. [5]And you have forgotten the exhortation which speaks to you as to sons:

"My son, do not despise the chastening of
    the LORD,
  Nor be discouraged when you are rebuked
    by Him;
[6]For whom the LORD loves He chastens,
  And scourges every son whom He receives."

[7]If you endure chastening, **God deals with you as with sons;** for what son is there whom a father does not chasten? [8]But if you are without chastening, of which all have become partakers, then you are illegitimate and not sons. [9]Furthermore, we have had human fathers who corrected us, and we paid them respect. Shall we not much more readily be in subjection to the Father of spirits and live? [10]For they indeed for a few days chastened us as seemed best to them, but He for our profit, that we may be partakers of His holiness. [11]Now no chastening seems to be joyful for the present, but painful; nevertheless, afterward it yields the peaceable fruit of righteousness to those who have been trained by it.

DISCOVERY

Explore the Bible reading by discussing these questions.

2. Why did Jesus accept the shame of the cross?

_____

_____

_____

3. What advice does this passage offer to those who are suffering?

_____

_____

_____

4. Whom does God discipline?

_____

_____

_____

5. Why does God allow his children to suffer?

_____

_____

_____

6. Why is it important to accept God's discipline?

_____

_____

_____

INSPIRATION

Here is an uplifting thought from the *Inspirational Study Bible.*

He looked around the carpentry shop. He stood for a moment in the refuge of the little room that housed so many sweet memories. He balanced the hammer in his hand. He ran his fingers across the sharp teeth of the saw. He stroked the smoothly worn wood of the sawhorse. He had come to say goodbye.

It was time for him to leave. He had heard something that made him know it was time to go. So he came one last time to smell the sawdust and lumber.

Life was peaceful here. Life was so . . . safe. . . .

I wonder if he wanted to stay. . . . I wonder because I know he had already read the last chapter. He knew that the feet that would step out of the safe shadow of the carpentry shop would not rest until they'd been pierced and placed on a Roman cross. . . .

If there was any hesitation on the part of his humanity, it was overcome by the compassion of his divinity. His divinity heard the voices. . . .

And his divinity saw the faces. . . . From the face of Adam to the face of the infant born somewhere in the world as you read these words, he saw them all.

And you can be sure of one thing. Among the voices that found their way into that carpentry shop in Nazareth was your voice. . . .

And not only did he hear you, he saw you. He saw your face aglow the hour you first knew him. He saw your face in shame the hour you first fell. The same face that looked back at you from this morning's mirror, looked at him. And it was enough to kill him.

He left because of you.

He laid his security down with his hammer. He hung tranquillity on the peg with his nail apron. He closed the window shutters on the sunshine of his youth and locked the door on the comfort and ease of anonymity.

Since he could bear your sins more easily than he could bear the thought of your hopelessness, he chose to leave.

It wasn't easy. Leaving the carpentry shop never has been.

(from *God Came Near*
by Max Lucado)

RESPONSE

Use these questions to share more deeply with each other.

7. How can thinking about Jesus' suffering help you face the pain in your life?

_____

_____

_____

8. In what specific ways does God discipline us?

_____

_____

_____

9. How can we learn to recognize and respond to God's correction in our lives?

_____

_____

_____

PRAYER

Father, forgive us for the times we have shaken our heads and pounded our fists against the earth and cried, "Why, God?" For Father, we know that when you allow us to suffer, you have our best interests at heart. Teach us to submit to your will instead of fighting for our own way. And in our darkest moments, remind us that you still love us.

JOURNALING

Take a few moments to record your personal insights from this lesson.

How has God's discipline improved my life and made me a more mature believer?

ADDITIONAL QUESTIONS

10. How does this passage challenge your attitude toward God's discipline?

_____

_____

_____

11. What might God be teaching you through some present difficulties?

_____

_____

_____

12. Why is it important to remember that God loves you even though he disciplines you?

_____

_____

_____

For more Bible passages about God's discipline, see Deuteronomy 4:36; 11:2–7; Job 5:17; Psalm 94:12; Proverbs 3:11; 10:17; Jeremiah 30:11; Hosea 5:1,2; Revelation 3:19.

To complete the book of Hebrews during this twelve-part study, read Hebrews 12:1–11.

ADDITIONAL THOUGHTS

LESSON ELEVEN

THE FEAR OF THE LORD

REFLECTION

Begin your study by sharing thoughts on this question.

1. Think of a person you greatly admire. How do you show your respect for
    that person?

_____

_____

_____

BIBLE READING

Read Hebrews 12:12–29 from the NCV or the NKJV.

NCV

¹²You have become weak, so make yourselves strong again. ¹³Live in the right way so
that you will be saved and your weakness will
not cause you to be lost.

¹⁴Try to live in peace with all people, and try
to live free from sin. Anyone whose life is not
holy will never see the Lord. ¹⁵Be careful that no
one fails to receive God's grace and begins to
cause trouble among you. A person like that can

NKJV

¹²Therefore strengthen the hands which
hang down, and the feeble knees, ¹³and make
straight paths for your feet, so that what is lame
may not be dislocated, but rather be healed.

¹⁴Pursue peace with all people, and holiness,
without which no one will see the Lord: ¹⁵look-
ing carefully lest anyone fall short of the grace
of God; lest any root of bitterness springing
up cause trouble, and by this many become

NCV

ruin many of you. [16]Be careful that no one takes part in sexual sin or is like Esau and never thinks about God. As the oldest son, Esau would have received everything from his father, but he sold all that for a single meal. [17]You remember that after Esau did this, he wanted to get his father's blessing, but his father refused. Esau could find no way to change what he had done, even though he wanted the blessing so much that he cried.

[18]You have not come to a mountain that can be touched and that is burning with fire. You have not come to darkness, sadness, and storms. [19]You have not come to the noise of a trumpet or to the sound of a voice like the one the people of Israel heard and begged not to hear another word. [20]They did not want to hear the command: "If anything, even an animal, touches the mountain, it must be put to death with stones." [21]What they saw was so terrible that Moses said, "I am shaking with fear."

[22]But you have come to Mount Zion, to the city of the living God, the heavenly Jerusalem. You have come to thousands of angels gathered together with joy. [23]You have come to the meeting of God's firstborn children whose names are written in heaven. You have come to God, the judge of all people, and to the spirits of good people who have been made perfect. [24]You have come to Jesus, the One who brought the new agreement from God to his people, and you have come to the sprinkled blood that has a better message than the blood of Abel.

[25]So be careful and do not refuse to listen when God speaks. Others refused to listen to him when he warned them on earth, and they

NKJV

defiled; [16]lest there be any fornicator or profane person like Esau, who for one morsel of food sold his birthright. [17]For you know that afterward, when he wanted to inherit the blessing, he was rejected, for he found no place for repentance, though he sought it diligently with tears.

[18]For you have not come to the mountain that may be touched and that burned with fire, and to blackness and darkness and tempest, [19]and the sound of a trumpet and the voice of words, so that those who heard it begged that the word should not be spoken to them anymore. [20] (For they could not endure what was commanded: "And if so much as a beast touches the mountain, it shall be stoned or shot with an arrow." [21]And so terrifying was the sight that Moses said, "I am exceedingly afraid and trembling.")

[22]But you have come to Mount Zion and to the city of the living God, the heavenly Jerusalem, to an innumerable company of angels, [23]to the general assembly and church of the firstborn who are registered in heaven, to God the Judge of all, to the spirits of just men made perfect, [24]to Jesus the Mediator of the new covenant, and to the blood of sprinkling that speaks better things than that of Abel.

[25]See that you do not refuse Him who speaks. For if they did not escape who refused Him who spoke on earth, much more shall we not escape if we turn away from Him who speaks from heaven, [26]whose voice then shook the earth; but now He has promised, saying, "Yet once more I shake not only the earth, but also heaven." [27]Now this, "Yet once more,"

NCV

did not escape. So it will be worse for us if we refuse to listen to God who warns us from heaven. ²⁶When he spoke before, his voice shook the earth, but now he has promised, "Once again I will shake not only the earth but also the heavens." ²⁷The words "once again" clearly show us that everything that was made—things that can be shaken—will be destroyed. Only the things that cannot be shaken will remain.

²⁸So let us be thankful, because we have a kingdom that cannot be shaken. We should worship God in a way that pleases him with respect and fear, ²⁹because our God is like a fire that burns things up.

NKJV

indicates the removal of those things that are being shaken, as of things that are made, that the things which cannot be shaken may remain.

²⁸Therefore, since we are receiving a kingdom which cannot be shaken, let us have grace, by which we may serve God acceptably with reverence and godly fear. ²⁹For our God is a consuming fire.

DISCOVERY

Explore the Bible reading by discussing these questions.

2. Why should Christians "live in the right way"?

_____

_____

_____

3. How can Christians avoid Esau's mistake?

_____

_____

_____

4. What difference has Jesus made in the way people know God?

_____

_____

_____

5. What will remain after God destroys this world?

_____

_____

_____

6. What kind of worship pleases God?

_____

_____

_____

INSPIRATION

Here is an uplifting thought from the *Inspirational Study Bible.*

The Bible says that, "The fear of the Lord is the beginning of wisdom." We don't fear Him as a tyrant but as a loving and just Father who leads us in wisdom and truth to do what is good for us, what will prolong and preserve our lives. But since God is a just Father, we know He will discipline and punish us when we defy Him and break His rules. If we break those rules often enough and carelessly enough, He will take our privileges away completely. That is the risk this world faces even now. . . .

Peace with God, the peace of God, and peace between nations is possible, if we repent of our sins, listen to Him, believe in Him, and follow Him. As servants, followers, brothers, and sisters of the Savior, we are commanded to be His allies in the cause of the true and lasting peace that He can bring. . . .

We are to expect the coming of Christ at any time, but we are to work as if He were not to come for a thousand years. . . .

In the meantime, we are to work for peace and harmony among the nations of the earth and to love our neighbors even as we love ourselves.

(from *Storm Warning* by Billy Graham)

RESPONSE

Use these questions to share more deeply with each other.

7. What does Scripture mean when it compares God to "a fire that burns things up"?

_____

_____

_____

8. What does it mean to fear God?

_____

_____

_____

9. How does the fear of the Lord affect your daily life?

_____

_____

_____

PRAYER

Dear Father, teach us what it means to worship you in reverence and awe. Purify us and make us holy as we eagerly wait for your unshakable kingdom to come to earth. Help us to see what is important, what is eternal, and what is lasting.

JOURNALING

Take a few moments to record your personal insights from this lesson.

How can I demonstrate reverence for God?

ADDITIONAL QUESTIONS

10. What can we learn from this passage about our future?

_____

_____

_____

11. If this world will be destroyed, how should we spend our time and energy?

_____

_____

_____

12. How does the way you spend your time reveal about your view of God?

_____   _____

_____

_____

For more Bible passages about fearing God, see Deuteronomy 6:13; 31:12, 13; 1 Samuel 12:14, 15; 2 Chronicles 19:7; Psalm 2:11; 19:9; 90:11; 147:11; Proverbs 1:7; 8:13; 10:27; Ecclesiastes 12:13, 14; Isaiah 33:6; Luke 12:5; 2 Corinthians 5:11; Revelation 14:7.

To complete the book of Hebrews during this twelve-part study, read Hebrews 12:12–29.

LESSON TWELVE

SERVING OTHERS

REFLECTION

Begin your study by sharing thoughts on this question.

1. When has a Christian brother or sister ministered to you in a meaningful way? How did this affect you?

_____

_____

_____

BIBLE READING

Read Hebrews 13:1–16 from the NCV or the NKJV.

NCV

¹Keep on loving each other as brothers and sisters. ²Remember to welcome strangers, because some who have done this have welcomed angels without knowing it. ³Remember those who are in prison as if you were in prison with them. Remember those who are suffering as if you were suffering with them.

⁴Marriage should be honored by everyone, and husband and wife should keep their

NKJV

¹Let brotherly love continue. ²Do not forget to entertain strangers, for by so doing some have unwittingly entertained angels. ³Remember the prisoners as if chained with them—those who are mistreated—since you yourselves are in the body also.

⁴Marriage is honorable among all, and the bed undefiled; but fornicators and adulterers God will judge.

NCV

marriage pure. God will judge as guilty those who take part in sexual sins. ⁵Keep your lives free from the love of money, and be satisfied with what you have. God has said,

"I will never leave you;
    I will never forget you."
⁶So we can be sure when we say,
    "I will not be afraid, because the Lord is my
        helper.
    People can't do anything to me."

⁷Remember your leaders who taught God's message to you. Remember how they lived and died, and copy their faith. ⁸Jesus Christ is the same yesterday, today, and forever.

⁹Do not let all kinds of strange teachings lead you into the wrong way. Your hearts should be strengthened by God's grace, not by obeying rules about foods, which do not help those who obey them.

¹⁰We have a sacrifice, but the priests who serve in the Holy Tent cannot eat from it. ¹¹The high priest carries the blood of animals into the Most Holy Place where he offers this blood for sins. But the bodies of the animals are burned outside the camp. ¹²So Jesus also suffered outside the city to make his people holy with his own blood. ¹³So let us go to Jesus outside the camp, holding on as he did when we are abused.

¹⁴Here on earth we do not have a city that lasts forever, but we are looking for the city that we will have in the future. ¹⁵So through Jesus let us always offer to God our sacrifice of praise, coming from lips that speak his name. ¹⁶Do not forget to do good to others, and share with them, because such sacrifices please God.

NKJV

⁵Let your conduct be without covetousness; be content with such things as you have. For He Himself has said, "I will never leave you nor forsake you." ⁶So we may boldly say:

"The LORD is my helper;
    I will not fear.
    What can man do to me?"

⁷Remember those who rule over you, who have spoken the word of God to you, whose faith follow, considering the outcome of their conduct. ⁸Jesus Christ is the same yesterday, today, and forever. ⁹Do not be carried about with various and strange doctrines. For it is good that the heart be established by grace, not with foods which have not profited those who have been occupied with them.

¹⁰We have an altar from which those who serve the tabernacle have no right to eat. ¹¹For the bodies of those animals, whose blood is brought into the sanctuary by the high priest for sin, are burned outside the camp. ¹²Therefore Jesus also, that He might sanctify the people with His own blood, suffered outside the gate. ¹³Therefore let us go forth to Him, outside the camp, bearing His reproach. ¹⁴For here we have no continuing city, but we seek the one to come. ¹⁵Therefore by Him let us continually offer the sacrifice of praise to God, that is, the fruit of our lips, giving thanks to His name. ¹⁶But do not forget to do good and to share, for with such sacrifices God is well pleased.

DISCOVERY

Explore the Bible reading by discussing these questions.

2. How should Christians show their love for one another?

_____

_____

_____

3. What responsibility do believers have to help people in need?

_____

_____

_____

4. What gives believers a sense of satisfaction and contentment?

_____

_____

_____

5. What is the future city described in this passage?

_____

_____

_____

6. What kind of sacrifices please God?

_____

_____

_____

INSPIRATION

Here is an uplifting thought from the *Inspirational Study Bible.*

Two great problems in serving others are both problems of human nature, of focusing on our relationship with people instead of our relationship with Christ. The first problem is that people will expect too much of you; and the second, you will expect too much of them. Both of these problems are problems of unrealistic expectations. Expectations must be focused on Christ, not each other. He is the only One who will consistently not let us down.

The milk of human sympathy will undernourish your soul. No amount of human gratitude will properly compensate your effort to improve the human condition. When we focus on serving the person, we are inevitably disappointed. And what's more, we will disappoint them. Serving people for the sake of their gratitude is a guaranteed formula for disappointment. Just when you begin to feel good about your labors, someone lets you down. Or, more likely, someone will expect too much from you and accuse you of letting them down. Either way, your destiny is to be terribly discouraged. . . .

The key is the personal relationship with Christ. The focus must not be on serving others or on being served. The focus must be on Jesus, on becoming so absorbed in the relationship with Him that every other thing is a response to our relationship. We don't serve men; we serve God. Have no expectations of men. Focus on the personal relationship with Him, and there will be an overflow available for others.

Look to Christ alone for gratitude. If you serve Christ, then you will remember to look to Him for your approval, not to the milk of human sympathy. He will reward you for serving others; in fact, He is the reward.

When someone feels you let them down, you can surrender that relationship to Christ. You are serving Him only; He will give you the strength to serve that person more. You may want to flee from the ingratitude—the insa-tiable demands of other people—but Christ will empower you to be a servant if you take on His attitude. It can only come by devotion to the personal relationship.

The personal relationship with Christ is the oasis in the desert of human relations. When people begin to wear you down, let it remind you that you are not in the overflow. It is time to drink of Christ.

(from *Walking with Christ
in the Details of Life*
by Patrick Morley)

RESPONSE

Use these questions to share more deeply with each other.

7. How has your relationship with Jesus changed the way you treat others?

_____

_____

_____

8. What problems arise in serving others?

_____

_____

_____

9. How can we avoid or deal with these problems?

_____

_____

_____

PRAYER

Father, thank you for the perfect example of Christ's humble service. Keep our eyes focused on you and protect us from selfish desires, ulterior motives, and unrealistic expectations. May your great love for us spur us on to love and serve one another.

JOURNALING

Take a few moments to record your personal insights from this lesson.

What humble act of service can I offer to God today?

ADDITIONAL QUESTIONS

10. What is the key to enjoying Christian service?

_____

_____

_____

11. What can you do when you feel discouraged about your ministry?

_____

_____

_____

12. How can you remind yourself to seek only Christ's approval for your service?

_____

_____

_____

For more Bible passages about serving, see Deuteronomy 10:12; 2 Chronicles 19:9; Psalm 2:11; Luke 12:35; 1 Corinthians 12:5; 16:15, 16; 2 Corinthians 9:12; Galatians 5:13; Ephesians 4:11–13; Colossians 3:23, 24; 1 Timothy 6:2; Revelation 2:19.

To complete the book of Hebrews during this twelve-part study, read Hebrews 13:1–25.

ADDITIONAL THOUGHTS

ADDITIONAL THOUGHTS

LEADERS' NOTES

LESSON ONE

Question 1: It's safe to answer, "my spouse," or "prayer." If no one gets honest, suggest some less honorable options, like food, a movie (escape), etc.

Question 3: Refer back to the prophecy in Genesis 3:14–15. Point out that this is what most people consider the first reference to the effect Christ would have on Satan.

Question 4: You might want to explore the fear of death before answering this question. Has anyone known someone who was terrified of dying? (Maybe someone *present* is.) What is he or she specifically afraid of? Then, when you start to discuss what frees us from that fear, you can relate it back to the specific fears mentioned.

Question 5: It might also help the discussion if you ask how Jesus' pain and temptation are *different* from our own.

LESSON TWO

Question 5: This is a great opportunity for discussion. Rather than giving short answers, like "disobedience" or "tragedy," take time to hear some actual stories about people whom the group members have known. Think ahead of time so you have a story to share to open the discussion.

Question 7: Be careful to maintain balance here. It's easy to get into a gender-related discussion about emotions. Because a person is emotional doesn't mean his/her faith is not real. Faith can lead to emotion. It just can't be based on emotion.

Question 8: Read James 2:14–17 (read through verse 26 if you don't mind a longer passage). Discuss current examples of faith without works.

Question 11: If you can, offer some examples of how your own life is different in proportion to the time you spend in fellowship with believers.

LESSON THREE

Question 3: If you need to deepen the discussion, broaden it to why even the faithful among us fail to be helped by the gospel at times.

Question 11: This is a vulnerable question. You might want to take the lead with your own response to let the group know that this is a time to be real.

LESSON FOUR

Question 1: If you're trying to loosen up the group you might ask a few fun questions like, "What's the hardest secret you've ever kept?" or "Does anyone here have a secret they've kept completely to themselves for a year? five years? ten years? more?"

Question 8: Try to have an answer ready, even if you're not particularly proud of it.

LESSON FIVE

Question 1: Spend some time on this as a way to get to know a little more about each others' past. If you have someone who will be reticent to share, see if you can do some homework by talking to him or her ahead of time and helping out (without causing any embarrassment, of course.)

Question 4: Many people have favorite verses about God's faithfulness; verses that have encouraged them in a hard time. Allow time for sharing some of those. Examples: Lamentations 3:23, Isaiah 41:10.

Question 5: Incorporate Proverbs 19:21 into this discussion. Ask if anyone has ever had great plans that fell through, but later, looking back, they could see God's purposes standing firm.

Question 6: A good follow-up question might be, Have you ever felt like God lied to you? How can you reconcile that with this passage?

Question 10: Proverbs 3:5–7 has a lot to add to this question.

Question 12: If it seems appropriate, ask about the situations your group members will be facing and, perhaps, even list them for prayer requests.

LESSON SIX

Question 1: If people seem hesitant to respond, give them the freedom to be ambiguous about what they needed forgiveness for.

Question 2: Some of your group members may be much more familiar with guilt than forgiveness. Be sensitive to that and, if necessary, work backward: How does it feel to be unforgiven?

Question 9: Psalm 103:12 says our sins are removed as far as the east is from the west. Even a sunrise can remind us that we are forgiven.

Question 10: This question will probably elicit responses relating to unworthiness and guilt. Also, explore with the group how pride affects our desire to be forgiven and our acceptance of God's forgiveness.

LESSON SEVEN

Question 7: This could be a long list. You might recall that a popular evangelist used this question to clarify the issue: "If you stand before God tonight and he says, 'Why should I let you in my heaven?' what would your answer be?"

Question 8: 1 John 3:19–20 says that even if our hearts condemn us and make us doubt our acceptance by God, we must remember, God is greater than our hearts.

Question 9: This is an excellent question to explore with the group. Take time. It is humbling at times to realize that our lives can become comfortable and we have days when Christ's death hasn't obviously affected us.

LESSON EIGHT

Question 1: If the group needs some warming up, ask for some light stories like, "Have you ever been the fool to rush in where angels fear to tread?"

Question 2: A picture of one of Christ's greatest accomplishments is found in Matthew 27:50–51. A curtain or veil in the temple blocked the way between the worshiper and the holiest of rooms where God dwelt. At Jesus' death, that curtain tore from top to bottom to give us access to God.

Question 12: Get specific. How can this group help each other?

LESSON NINE

Question 1: Rather than just getting the facts, take the time to hear about those significant people who have touched each of you. What are their names? Discuss them with each other.

Question 3: Now take a good look at these people. They were people who made mistakes. Sarah laughed at God's promise. Abraham lied about Sarah being his wife. Noah got drunk and acted inappropriately. Focus on their faith in God, not their own goodness. They were not super human.

Question 12: Share some prayer requests. What do you need faith to do? What risks do you need to take?

LESSON TEN

Question 2: Philippians 2:4–8 says one reason Christ endured the cross is that he put our interests above his own.

Question 5: Can you think of any parallel reasons why a parent would let his or her child suffer? For example, separation anxiety: leaving a child in the nursery when he or she is crying; allowing a child to suffer when being treated for illness. Some battles are the child's to fight.

Question 10: Depending on your group, it might be a surprise to some that God's goal is not to make our every moment a happy one. Take time to discuss this if it comes up.

LESSON ELEVEN

Question 3: Delayed gratification was something Esau was not willing to accept. That definitely relates to our society today.

Question 6: John 4:23, 24 tells us what kind of worshipers the Father seeks. They worship in spirit and in truth.

Question 9: Another way to ask this is, "What would you do differently if you didn't fear God?"

LESSON TWELVE

Question 8: If it comes up in the discussion, talk about the balance between being responsible for taking care of ourselves and forgetting ourselves to serve others. Is that balance an easy one for this group?

Question 10: Burnout is a big issue in service, both professional and volunteer ministry. How can you keep from burning out?

Question 12: In what places of service is it easiest to be a people pleaser?

ADDITIONAL NOTES

ADDITIONAL NOTES

ADDITIONAL NOTES

ADDITIONAL NOTES

ADDITIONAL NOTES

ADDITIONAL NOTES

ACKNOWLEDGMENTS

Graham, Billy. *Peace with God*, copyright 1985, W Publishing Group, Nashville, TN

Graham, Billy. *Storm Warning*, copyright 1986, W Publishing Group, Nashville, TN

Graham, Billy. *Unto the Hills*, copyright 1986, W Publishing Group, Nashville, TN

Lucado, Max. *The Applause of Heaven*, copyright 1990, W Publishing Group, Nashville, TN

Lucado, Max. *God Came Near*, Questar Publishers, Multnomah Books, copyright 1987 by Max Lucado.

Lucado, Max. *He Still Moves Stones*, copyright 1993, W Publishing Group, Nashville, TN

Lucado, Max. *On the Anvil*, copyright 1985 by Max Lucado. Used by permission of Tyndale House Publishers, Inc. All rights reserved.

Lucado, Max. *Six Hours One Friday*, Questar Publishers, Multnomah Books, copyright 1989 by Max Lucado.

Morley, Patrick. *Walking with Christ in the Details of Life*, copyright 1992 by Thomas Nelson, Nashville, Tennessee.